Purchased with funds
donated to the
Huron County Library

S0-BRT-713

DISCARD

971.61404092 Haine

Haines, M.
The spitting champion of the
world.

PRICE: $30.00 (3559/cl   )

DISCARD

THE SPITTING CHAMPION OF THE WORLD

MEMORIES OF ANTIGONISH

ALSO BY MAX HAINES

Bothersome Bodies

Calendar of Criminal Capers

Crime Flashback #1

Crime Flashback #2

Crime Flashback #3

The Murderous Kind

Murder & Mayhem

The Collected Works of Max Haines, Volume 1

That's Life

True Crime Stories

True Crime Stories, Book II

True Crime Stories, Book III

True Crime Stories, Book IV

The Collected Works of Max Haines, Volume 2

True Crime Stories, Book V

Doctors Who Kill

Multiple Murderers

Multiple Murderers II

Celebrity Murders

The Collected Works of Max Haines, Volume 3

Murders Strange but True

Canadian Crimes

Murder Most Foul

The Collected Works of Max Haines, Volume 4

Unnatural Causes

Instruments of Murder

The Collected Works of Max Haines, Volume 5